Marinella Pashova

BULGARIAN 4 BRITS

Listen and repeat language guide

Part 1

Propmags Publishing
UK

Published in United Kingdom by:

Propmags Publishing

PO Box 1113
Southampton
SO16 6XH
England

www.bulgarian4brits.com

First published August 2005
Reprinted June 2006

ISBN   0-9550711-0-0

Dear reader,

This language guide should be the easiest way for you to start speaking and understanding Bulgarian. I have drawn on my experience in teaching and have taken into account the pace, learning style and needs of my students. Based on this and some additional research, I have created this product to meet your needs. It's designed according to the speed, format and topics range that you actually need, to take your first steps in Bulgarian.

To achieve best learning results, my advice is- listen to the CDs as often as you can, try and repeat as much as you can, and do study the Cyrillic's- you will soon see the benefits.

If something slips- just go back. Don't give up!

I will be with you all the way!

Marinella Pashova - Melly

**A big thank you to all those, without whom the creation
of this product wouldn't have been possible.**

Product manager: Sabina Pashova

The book

Editors: Simon Clark and Sabina Pashova
Cover design: Karen Hodgson
Illustrations: Darren Mullen

The CD

English vocals: Darren Prosser
Bulgarian male vocals: Chavdar Gergov

Recording: Studio "RAY" Sofia, Bulgaria
Sound engineer: Angel Popov

Studio "Sound on Sound" UK

Printed in Sofia, Bulgaria by MITRA PR

Bulgarian female vocals and vocals in the closing track: Marinella Pashova

CONTENTS

Introduction

The bit about the Author

Marinella Pashova (Melly) was born in Bulgaria in the city of Pernik. She graduated Bulgarian philology at Sofia University and taught Bulgarian language and literature to high school students for several years.

In the UK in 2004, Melly founded a pioneering dedicated group for Bulgarian tuition to Brits, who had bought properties in Bulgaria.

She has first hand experience with teaching British house-hunters Bulgarian and has an exact idea what level of detail and range of topics are most necessary and appropriate.

Where it all started

The classes have been very successful and have inspired Melly to develop this manual to try and reach the thousands of British people, who need to learn just enough to help them during their stay in Bulgaria.

What really spun the project was a call out for such product, from many forum members on "My Bulgaria"-the number one website for advice and information, dedicated to British people, who have investment interest in Bulgaria. This product comes to market genuinely born from this demand and in answer to the speck from you- the very people who need it.

The bit about the book

This language guide is inspired by the newly emerged British interest in Bulgaria and it's targeted and specifically designed for those, who are new to the language, who need to learn some basic things, but don't want to get too involved with the grammar. If this sounds like you- then you are in the right place!

The book is accompanied by two CDs, which will be of incredible value to you, as you can accustom your self to the sound of the language, repeat and learn a lot of basic, but essential everyday Bulgarian phrases and words. The manual does not set out to teach you the grammatical structure of the Bulgarian language, but instead helps you to handle common situations, that you will encounter as a visitor or a part time resident in Bulgaria. You will learn how to ask for what you need, to do your grocery shopping, to request information and express yourself at a basic level.

The value of the manual is in its simplicity, the topics covered and of course, particularly in the benefit that listening to the CDs will give you in your efforts.

How does it work?

This manual contains 10 lessons, covering important and useful toppics, which should enable you to gain basic understanding of the phrases, you will need to use and you are likely to hear in these situations.

In the chapter introducing the Bulgarian alphabet, you will see all the letters and hear all the sounds of the alphabet. For your ease and the benefit of your pronunciation, they are all transcribed and these transcriptions are used all along all the phrases throughout the book.

A short dictionary, following the lessons sequence is provided at the back.

For the purposes of studying the language the CD's are audio only.
However, after the lessons there is an interactive CDR section, containing an extensive interactive dictionary and some useful links.

Each lesson is split to the following sections:

Dialogue one (audio accompanied)- listen and repeat

A short, very basic conversation, read first in Bulgarian only. After that, the separate phrases are said first in English and then - slowly in Bulgarian, followed by gaps for repetition.

Dialogue two (audio accompanied) - listen and repeat

A further conversation, on a similar subject and principle as the first one.

Section MORE... (audio accompanied)- listen and repeat

Phrases from the text are taken out and different uses and combinations are offered, to allow you to construct your own sentences and grasp the semantics of single words.

Section AND MORE... (audio accompanied) - listen and repeat

This section offers further detail for you to practice on, still in relation with the text above.

READ ME! section (not accompanied by audio)

This part is looking at some very simplified grammar highlights, just to enable you to get over the basics of using and understanding the language. It is really worth reading through these sections- it will make all the difference to your understanding.

Exercises (audio only)

Short, useful and basic exercises, giving you the opportunity to ask questions and give answers, while testing your understanding, hence building your confidence to talk and converse.

In the accompanying CDs, each lesson is a separate track, where the number of the tracks and these of the lessons match for your convenience.
Track one contains a short introduction and the Bulgarian alphabet as well as lesson one.

ΛБВ...

The Bulgarian alphabet

The Bulgarian alphabet consists of 30 letters, each represented by one consistent sound. Once you have learned all the letters, you can then pronounce any word, it's easy.

For your benefit special, specific transcription characters have been introduced for every letter and sound, which you will meet throughout the book. Remember them well, as they will help you pronounce all the words that follow- correctly. Whenever you forget some - always come back to this lesson.

Don't only rely on the transcription, but try to learn the Cyrillics, as you will need them, particularly if you intend to spend longer in Bulgaria.

Letters	Sound	English Examples	Bulgarian examples
А а	ah	**as in a**rt, Arnold	ало, апетит ah-loh, ah-peh-tit
Б б	b	**b**ook, **B**ob	бар, Балкан bar, bal-kan
В в	v	**v**ane, **V**ivian	вода, вана voh-dah, vah-nah
Г г	g	**g**ood, **G**ordon	голям, говоря goh-lyam, goh-voh-ryah
Д д	d	**d**eep, **D**avid	добре, да dob-reh, dah
Е е	eh	**e**lse, **E**mma	ела!, елен eh-lah, eh-len

Letters	Sound	English Examples	Bulgarian examples
Ж ж	j	leisure , **Zh**ivago	жена, живот
			jeh-nah,jih-vot
З з	z	**z**ip, **Z**orro	зима, земя
			zih-mah, zeh-myah
И и	ih	**i**nnocent, **I**an	има, име
			ih-mah, ih-meh
Й й	y	**y**es, Gu**y**	йод, Йордания
			yod, yor-dah-nih-yah
К к	k	**k**ind, **K**aren	кога, какво
			koh-gah, kak-voh
Л л	l	**l**emon, **L**indsey	леко, лято
			leh-koh, lyah-toh
М м	m	**m**oon, **M**ike	мама, магазин
			mah-mah, mah-gah-zin
Н н	n	**n**ever, **N**ick	не, няма
			neh, nyah-mah
О о	oh	**o**ffice, **O**liver	обичам, осем
			oh-bih-cham, oh-sem
П п	p	**p**ork, **P**eter	пари, пия
			pah-rih, pih-yah
Р р	r /rolled as Scotish "r"/	British, **R**ambo	радост, работа
			rah-dost, rah-boh-tah
С с	s	**s**ummer, **S**imon	слънце, стая
			sluhn-zeh, stah-yah
Т т	t	**t**ime, **T**om	това, толкова
			toh-vah, tol-koh-vah

Letters	Sound	English Examples	Bulgarian examples
У у	ooh /but shorter/	foot, Uma	урок, уча ooh-rok, ooh-chah
Ф ф	f	fantastic, Fiona	фар, финал far, fih-nal
Х х	H	hobby, Harry	хубаво, хляб Hooh-bah-voh, Hlyab
Ц ц	ts	fits, tsar	целувам, цвете tseh-luh-vam, tsveh-teh
Ч ч	ch	chair, Charly	червено, червило cher-veh-noh, cher-vih-loh
Ш ш	sh	shop, Sharon	шунка, шофьор shun-kah, shoh-fior
Щ щ	sht	ashtray, Ashton	щастие, ще shtas-tih-eh, shteh
Ъ ъ	uh	urgent, Earnest	ъгъл, България uh-guhl, Buhl-gah-rih-yah

Ь ь - non pronounceable. Softens the preceding consonant

Letters	Sound	English Examples	Bulgarian examples
Ю ю	iu	universe, Yootha	юрист, юли iuh-rist, iuh-lih
Я я	ya	yard, Yahoo	ям, ябълка yam, yah-buhl-kah

LESSON 1

Meet and greet

Dialogue 1

Good afternoon!
Добър ден!
Doh-buhr den!

Hello!
Здравей!
Zdrah-veyh!

How are you?
Как си?
Kak sih?

Fine, thank you!
Благодаря, добре!
Blah-goh-dah-ryah, dob-reh!

What is your name?
Как се казваш?
Kak seh kaz-vash?

My name is Ivan, and yours?
Казвам се Иван, а ти?
Kaz-vam seh Ih-van, ah tih?

My name is Maria! My pleasure!
Аз се казвам Мария! Приятно ми е!
Az seh kaz-vam Mah-rih-yah! Prih-yat-noh mih eh !

Mine too!
И на мен!
Ih nah men!

Dialogue 2

Excuse me, do you speak Bulgarian?
Извинете, говорите ли български?
Izh-vih-neh-teh, goh-voh-rih-teh lih buhl-gar-skih?

Sorry? Speak slowly, please!
Моля? Говорете бавно!
Moh-lyah? Goh-voh-reh-teh bav-noh!

Do you speak Bulgarian?
Говорите ли български?
Goh-voh-rih-teh lih buhl-gar-skih?

Yes, but not very well. And you?
Да, но не много добре! А Вие?
Dah, noh neh mnoh-goh dob-reh! Ah vieh?

Yes. I speak Bulgarian well!
Да. Аз говоря български добре!
Dah. Az goh-voh-ryah buhl-gar-skih dob-reh!

Where are you from?
Вие от къде сте?
Vih-eh ot kuh-deh steh?

From Bulgaria. I am Bulgarian, and you?
От България. Аз съм българка, а Вие?
Ot Buhl-gah-rih-yah. Az suhm buhl-gar-kah, ah vih-eh?

I am from England. I'm English.
Аз съм от Англия. Англичанин съм.
Az suhm ot An-glih-yah. An-glih-chah-nin suhm.

14

Do you speak Bulgarian?
Говорите ли български?
Goh-voh-rih-teh lih buhl-gar-skih?

No. I do not speak Bulgarian. I don't understand.
Не. Не говоря български. Не разбирам!
Neh. Neh goh-voh-ryah buhl-gar-skih. Neh raz-bih-ram.

Good bye, have a nice day!
Довиждане, приятен ден!
Doh-vij-dah-neh, prih-yah-ten den!

Good bye and all the best!
Довиждане и всичко хубаво!
Doh-vij-dah-neh ih vsich-koh Hooh-bah-voh!

MORE...

Good evening!
Добър вечер!
Doh-buhr veh-cher!

Good morning!
Добро утро!
Dob-roh ooht-roh!

Good night!
Лека нощ!
Leh-kah nosht!

Welcome!
Добре дошли!
Dohb-reh dosh-lih!

Have a good evening!
Приятна вечер!
Pih-yat-nah veh-cher!

Have a nice time!
Приятно прекарване!
Prih-yat-noh preh-kar-vah-neh!

Have a good day at work!
Приятна работа!
Prih-yat-nah rah-boh-tah!

AND MORE...

Excuse me, do you speak English?
Извинете, говорите ли английски?
Iz-vih-neh-teh, goh-voh-rih-teh lih an-gliyh-skih?

No, I don't understand!
Не, не разбирам!   НЕ РАЗБИРАМ
Neh, neh-raz-bih-ram!

Where are you from?
Вие от къде сте?
Vih-eh ot kuh-deh steh?

I am from America. I am American.
Аз съм от Америка. Американец съм.
Az suhm ot Ah-meh-rih-kah. Ah-meh-rih-kah-nets suhm

Are you an English woman?
Вие англичанка ли сте?
Vih-eh an-glih-chan-kah lih steh?

Yes, I am an English woman. I am from England!
Да, англичанка съм. Аз съм от Англия.
Dah, an-glih-chan-kah suhm. Az suhm ot An-glih-yah.

Are you Scottish?
Вие шотландец ли сте?
Vih-eh shot-lan-dets lih steh?

No, I am not Scottish.
Не, не съм шотландец.
Neh, neh suhm shot-lan-dets.

16

I am from Ireland. I am an Irishman.
Аз съм от Ирландия. Ирландец съм.

Az suhm ot Ir-lan-dih-yah. Ir-lan-dets suhm.

READ ME!

Genders

In Bulgarian language there are 3 genders to nouns - feminine, masculine and neuter. These apply to all things - living or not and the adjectives describing them, agree with their gender when used together in a sentence.

As a very general rule, they end as shown below, but as with every rule, there are exceptions:

Feminine: **-а/-я**   хубав**а** мас**а**, земя**я**

Masculine: a **consonant** or **-й**   хуба**в** мъ**ж**, геро**й**, чужденец**ц**

Neuter: **-е/-и/-о**   хубав**о** мор**е**, такс**и**, писм**о**

Please note, the neuter gender applies not only to things as in English, but also to people (and animals), like "child" and "dog", for example.

The adverb "Добре"

The adverb "Добре" is used often and in slightly different ways. It adopts a different meaning, depending on the phrase. Below are some of the most common examples for you:

Добре - well
> - Аз се чувствам добре. - I feel well.

Добре - OK (an agreement; understood)
> - Добре, съгласен съм. - OK, I agree, I see...

Добре - approval - good
> - Добре! - Good! Well done!

The adjective "Добър" - in the three genders:

Добър (m), добра (f), добро (n)

> - добъ**р** ден
>> Good afternoon (Good day)

> - добр**о** утро
>> Good morning

> - добр**а** майка
>> Good mother

Listening exercises. (CD only)

LESSON 2

I am...

Dialogue 1

/to be/

Hello, I am a tourist!
Здравей, **аз съм** турист!
Zdrah-veyh, az suhm tooh-rist.

Hello, you are a tourist, are you? And he?
Здрасти, **ти си** турист, така ли? А той?
Zdras-tih, tih sih tooh-rist, tah-kah lih? Ah toyh?

He is a foreigner, and her?
Той е чужденец, а тя?
Toyh eh choohj-deh-nets, ah tyah?

She is a foreigner. And it?
Тя е чужденка. А то?
Tyah eh choohj-den-kah. A h toh?

It is a dog!
То е куче!
Toh eh kooh-cheh!

We are friends, you are a family. And they?
Ние сме приятели, **вие сте** семейство. А те?
Nieh smeh prih-yah-teh-lih, vieh steh seh-meys-tvoh.
Ah teh?

They are colleagues.
Те са колеги.
Teh sah koh-leh-gih.

Dialogue 2

/I have/

Hello Maria, how are you?
Здравей Мария, как си?
Zdrah-veyh Mah-rih-yah, kak sih?

Hi Ivan, I am fine, and you?
Здрасти Иване, добре съм, а ти?
Zdras-tih Ih-vah-neh, dob-reh suhm, ah tih?

I am fine too!
И аз съм добре!
Ih az suhm dob-reh!

Do you have a house in Bulgaria?
Имаш ли къща в България?
Ih-mash lih kuhsh-tah v Buhl-gah-rih-yah?

Yes, I have! I have one house.
Да, **имам**! Аз имам една къща.
Dah, Ih-mam ! Az ih-mam ed-nah kuhsh-tah!

We have two houses.
Ние **имаме** две къщи.
Nie ih-mah-meh dveh kuhsh-tih.

Paul has three houses.
Пол **има** три къщи.
Pohl ih-mah trih kuhsh-tih.

Lisa has ten houses.
Лиса **има** десет къщи.
Lisa ih-mah deh-set kuhsh-tih.

We have ten houses too!
И ние **имаме** десет къщи!
Ih nieh ih-mah-meh deh-set kuhsh-tih!

You also have many houses!
Вие също **имате** много къщи!
Vih-eh sush-toh ih-mah-teh mnoh-goh kuhsh-tih!

Oh, they have many houses!
О, те **имат** много къщи!
Oh, teh ih-mat mnoh-goh kuhsh-tih!

MORE...

I - **Аз** /Az/

you - **Ти** /Tih/

He -**Той** /Toyh /
She - **Тя** /Tyah/
It - **То** /Toh/

We - **Ние** / Nih-eh/

You - **Вие** /Vih-eh/

They - **Те** /Teh/

AND MORE...

/I am/

I am fine.
Аз съм добре.
Az suhm dob-reh.

You are tired.
Ти си уморен.
Tih sih ooh-moh-ren.

She is pretty.
Тя е хубава.
Tyah eh Hooh-bah-vah.

We are in Sofia.
Ние сме в София.
Nieh smeh v Soh-fih-yah.

You are neighbours.
Вие сте съседи.
Vieh steh suh-seh-dih.

They are good.
Те са добри.
Teh sah dob-rih.

Numbers 1-10

1- едно /ed-noh/
2- две /dveh/
3- три /trih/
4- четири /cheh-tih-rih/
5- пет /peht/
6- шест /shest/
7- седем /seh-dem/
8- осем /oh-sem/
9- девет /deh-vet/
10- десет /deh-set/

READ ME!

Out of all numbers, only the number **one** in Bulgarian has three genders:

Един - (m) Един коридор - one corridor

Една - (f) Една спалня- one bedroom

Едно - (n) Едно легло- one bed

The masculine form for example is used for the time i.e.: Един часа. - One O'clock.

The number **two** has a special form for masculine gender, which is **два:** Два часа. - Two O'clock.

The pronoun "Вие"

The pronoun "**Вие**" in the form for second person plural, is also used in Bulgarian to address formally one person. It is a polite way of approaching a person of authority or seniority or generally people we don't know in person i.e.

Вие сте Доктор. - You are a doctor.

In this use it is always written with a capital letter:

Listening exercises. (CD only)

LESSON 3

In the shop

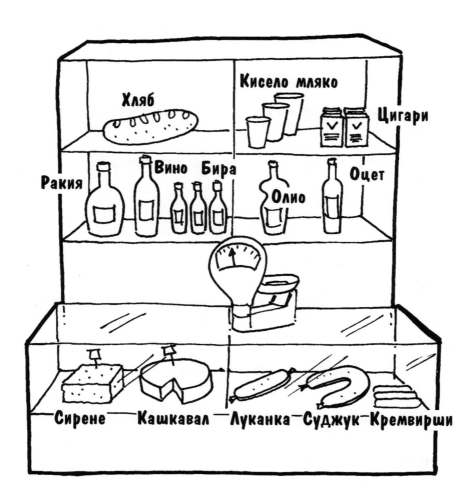

Хляб

Кисело мляко

Цигари

Ракия   Вино   Бира   Оцет

Олио

Сирене — Кашкавал — Луканка — Суджук — Кремвирши

Dialogue 1

Good afternoon. What would you like, please?
Добър ден, какво ще обичате моля?
Doh-buhr den, kak-voh shteh obih-chah-teh moh-lyah?

Is there any bread?
Има ли хляб?
Ih-mah lih Hlyab?

There is! It's very nice!
Има! Много е хубав!
Imah! Mnoh-goh eh Hooh-bav!

Can I have one?
Може ли един?
Moh-jeh lih eh-din!

There we are!
Моля, заповядайте!
Moh-lyah, zah-poh-vyah-dayh-teh!

Thank you!
Благодаря!
Blah-goh-dah-ryah!

What is this?
Това какво е?
Toh-vah kak-voh eh?

Yoghurt.
Кисело мляко.
Kih-seh-loh mlyah-koh.

How much does it cost?
Колко струва?
Kol-koh strooh-vah?

One lev.
Един лев.
Eh-din lev.

Give me three.
Дайте ми три!
Dayh-teh mih trih!

Dialogue 2

Excuse me, do you have any wine?
Извинете, имате ли вино?
Iz-vih-neh-teh, ih-ma-teh lih vih-noh?

No, there isn't any!
Не, няма!
Neh, nyah-mah!

How much does a beer cost?
Колко струва една бира?
Kol-koh strooh-vah ed-nah bih-rah?

Two leva!
Два лева!
Dvah leh-vah!

Can I have five beers!
Може ли пет бири!
Moh-jeh lih pet bih-rih!

Yes! Ten leva all together, please!
Да! Общо десет лева, моля!
Dah! Ob-shtoh deh-set leh-vah, moh-lyah!

Here we are!
Заповядайте!
Zah-poh-vyah-dayh-teh!

Thank you! Bye-bye!
Благодаря, довиждане!
Blah-goh-dah-ryah, doh-vij-dah-neh!

MORE...

Can I have one packet of cigarettes?
Може ли една кутия цигари?
Moh-jeh lih ed-nah kooh-tih-yah tsih-gah-rih?

Here you go!
Заповядайте!
Zah-poh-vyah-dayh-teh!

Can I get through / past?
Може ли да мина?
Moh-jeh lih dah mih-nah?

Yes, you can.
Да, **може**.
Dah, moh-jeh.

Can I ask..?
Може ли да питам...?
Moh-jeh lih dah pih-tam...?

There you go!
Заповядайте!
Zah-poh-vyah-dayh-teh!

29

Can I kiss you?
Може ли да те целуна?
Moh-jeh lih dah teh tseh-looh-nah?

No, you can't!
Не, **не може**!
Neh, neh moh-jeh!

AND MORE...

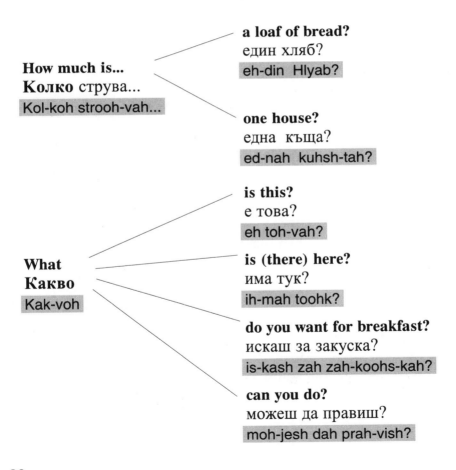

How much is...
Колко струва...
Kol-koh strooh-vah...

a loaf of bread?
един хляб?
eh-din Hlyab?

one house?
една къща?
ed-nah kuhsh-tah?

What
Какво
Kak-voh

is this?
е това?
eh toh-vah?

is (there) here?
има тук?
ih-mah toohk?

do you want for breakfast?
искаш за закуска?
is-kash zah zah-koohs-kah?

can you do?
можеш да правиш?
moh-jesh dah prah-vish?

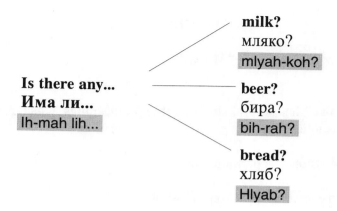

Is there any...
Има ли...
Ih-mah lih...

milk?
мляко?
mlyah-koh?

beer?
бира?
bih-rah?

bread?
хляб?
Hlyab?

MORE NUMBERS...

11 - единадесет / eh-dih-nah-deh-set /
12 - дванадесет / dvah-nah-deh-set /
13 - тринадесет / trih-nah-deh-set /

...

20 - двадесет / dvah-deh-set /
21 - двадесет и едно / dvah-deh-set ih ed-noh /
22 - двадесет и две / dvah-deh-set ih dveh /
23 - двадесет и три / dvah-deh-set ih trih /

...

30 - тридесет / trih-deh-set /
40 - четиридесет / cheh-tih-rih-deh-set /
50 - петдесет / pet-deh-set /
100 - сто / stoh /

READ ME!

"Може"

The word **"може"** has several slightly different meanings, which can be described as follows:

може- as permission, it's permitted to:

> Може да пушите. - You can smoke.

може- as probability, could, may :

> Може да те видя по късно. - I may see you later.

може- as capability- able to:

> Иван може да шофира.- Ivan can (is able to) drive.

Other common uses of the word "може" are:

може би -may be

може ли?- A question: Is it possible?

> Може ли да дойда по-късно?- Can I come later?

може ли?- as a polite request, Could?

> Може ли да питам? - Could I ask?

Forming numbers 10-100

Numbers 10 to 20 are formed in the following way:

Directly translated: small number **on** ten.

12 - два- **на** десет = дванадесет
17 - седем-**на**-десет = седемнадесет

Round numbers 20 - 90

The round numbers from 20- 90 are formed by simply putting the small
number directly in front of the word "десет"/ten/

20 - два-десет = двадесет
60 - шест-десет = шестдесет

Interim numbers 20-99

The numbers between the round ones- the interim numbers are formed
in Bulgarian in the following manner:

It literally translates into English as:

(Round number) and (small number)

25 - двадесет-**и**-пет = двадесет и пет

93 - деветдесет-**и**-три = деветдесет и три

Listening exercises. (CD only)

LESSON 4

OUT AND ABOUT

Dialogue 1

Excuse me, how can I get to the Post office?
Извинете, как да стигна до Пощата?
Iz-vih-neh-teh, kak dah stig-nah doh posh-tah-tah?

Carry on straight-ahead,
Продължете направо,
Proh-duhl-jeh-teh nah-prah-voh,

Right!
Така!
Tah-kah!

At the traffic lights turn right,
На светофара завийте надясно,
Nah sveh-toh-fah-rah zah-viyh-teh nah-dyas-noh,

and then left.
а след това наляво.
ah sled toh-vah nah-lyah-voh.

Is it far from here?
Далече ли е от тук?
Dah-leh-cheh lih eh ot toohk?

It's very close!
Много е близко!
Mnoh-goh eh bliz-koh!

It is situated at the end of the street.
Намира се в края на улицата.
Nah-mih-rah seh v krah-yah nah ooh-lih-tsah-tah.

Thanks a lot!
Благодаря много!
Blah-goh-dah-ryah mnoh-goh!

Pleasure!
Моля!
Moh-lyah!

Dialogue 2

Excuse me, where is the bank?
Извинете, къде е Банката?
Iz-vih-neh-teh , kuh-deh eh Ban-kah-tah ?

Go back,
Върнете се обратно,
Vuhr-neh-teh seh ob-rat-noh,

OK,
Добре,
Dob-reh,

Then cross the road.
След това пресечете улицата.
Sled toh-vah preh-seh-cheh-teh ooh-lih-tsah-tah.

Yeah,
Така,
Tah-kah,

There is a parking space there, and opposite it is the bank.
Там има паркинг, а срещу него е Банката.
Tam ih-mah par-king, ah sresh-tooh neh-goh eh ban-kah-tah.

Thank you very much!
Много Ви благодаря!
Mnoh-goh vih blah-goh-dah-ryah!

No problem, good luck.
Моля, успех!
Moh-lyah, oohs-peh!

MORE…

Excuse me,...
Извинете,...
Iz-vih-neh-teh,…

...where is the Post office?
...къде е пощата?
...kuh-deh eh posh-tah-tah?

I don't know!
Не знам!
Neh znam!

...where is the bank situated?
...къде се намира банката?
…kuh-deh seh nah-mih-rah
ban-kah-tah?

The bank is close.
Банката е близо.
Ban-kah-tah eh
blih-zoh.

...where is the Coach station?
...къде е автогарата?
…kuh-deh eh av-toh-gah-rah-tah?

Right opposite.
Точно отсреща.
Toch-noh ot-sreh-shtah

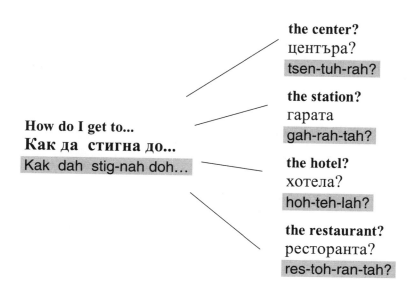

How do I get to...
Как да стигна до...
Kak dah stig-nah doh...

the center?
центъра?
tsen-tuh-rah?

the station?
гарата
gah-rah-tah?

the hotel?
хотела?
hoh-teh-lah?

the restaurant?
ресторанта?
res-toh-ran-tah?

AND MORE...

Where are you going?
Къде отиваш?
Kuh-deh oh-tih-vash?

To the beach.
На плаж.
Nah plaj.

Where is your house?
Къде е твоята къща?
Kuh-deh eh tvoh-yah-tah kush-tah?

In Rila
В Рила.
V Rih-lah.

Where do you hurt?
Къде те боли?
Kuh-deh teh boh-lih?

Here, in the back
Тук, на гърба.
Toohk, nah guhr-bah.

Where are we having dinner?
Къде ще вечеряме?
Kuh-deh shteh veh-cheh-ryah-meh?

In the restaurant.
В ресторанта.
V res-toh-ran-tah.

READ ME!

"Моля"

The word **" Моля"** is one of the most commonly used words in Bulgarian language and is applied in many situations.

Моля, is used in the following few nuances:

Моля - as a request, begging, pleading - as in "Please".

Моля за помощ! - I am asking for help!

Моля за внимание! - Please can I have your attention!

Моля - as a question, when we have not understood or heard something - as in "Pardon"?

Моля? Не разбрах, повторете. -
Pardon? I didn't understand, please repeat.

Моля - as a reply to thank you, as in "You are welcome."

А: Благодаря за помощта ви! - Thank you for your help!

Б: Моля! - You are welcome!

Listening exercises. (CD only)

LESSON 5

Travelling around

At the bus station

Excuse me, is this where the bus to Rila departs from?
Извинете, от тук ли тръгва рейсът за Рила?
Izvih-neh-teh, ot toohk li truhg-vah reyh-suht zah Rih-lah?

Yes.
Да.
Dah.

When?
Кога?
Koh-gah?

In half an hour.
След половин час.
Sled poh-loh-vin chas.

What is the time now?
Колко е часът сега?
Kol-koh eh chah-suht seh-gah?

Now is three O'clock!
Сега е три часа!
Seh-gah eh trih chah-sah!

How much is one ticket?
Колко струва един билет?
Kol-koh strooh-vah eh-din bih-let?

There and back, is that what you want?
Отиване и връщане ли искате?
Oh-tih-vah-neh ih vruhsh-tah-neh lih is-kah-teh?

I would like only one way, please!
Искам само отиване, моля!
Is-kam sah-moh oh-tih-vah-neh, moh-lyah!

It costs one lev.
Струва един лев.
Strooh-vah eh-din lehv.

Give me two tickets.
Дайте ми два билета.
Daih-teh mih dvah bih-leh-tah.

There you go!
Заповядайте!
Zah-poh-vyah-dayh-teh!

Thank you!
Благодаря!
Blah-goh-dah-ryah!

Dialogue 2

In the taxi

Hello, are you free?
Добър ден! Свободен ли сте?
Doh-buhr den! Svoh-boh-den lih steh?

Yes! Where are you going to?
Да! За къде сте?
Dah! Zah kuh-deh steh?

To hotel Sofia.
За хотел"София" .
Zah Hoh-tel "Soh-fih-yah".

OK!
Добре!
Dob-reh!

Would you stop here, please?
Спрете тук, моля!
Spreh-teh tuk, moh-lyah!

Done!
Готово!
Goh-toh-voh!

How much do I owe you?
Колко Ви дължа?
Kol-koh vih duhl-jah?

Six leva and seventy eight stotinki. (6.78)
Шест лева и седемдесет и осем стотинки. (6.78)
Shest leh-vah ih seh-dem-deh-set ih oh-sem stoh-tin-kih.

Could you repeat please!
Повторете, моля?
Pov-toh-reh-teh, moh-lyah?

Six leva and seventy eight stotinki. (6.78)
Шест лева и седемдесет и осем стотинки. (6.78)
Shest leh-vah ih seh-dem-deh-set ih oh-sem stoh-tin-kih.

Here you are! Keep the change!
Заповядайте! Задръжте рестото!
Zah-poh-vyah-dayh-teh! Zah-druhj-teh res-toh-toh!

Thank you!
Благодаря!
Blah-goh-dah-ryah!

OK, that's fine!
Моля, моля!
Moh-lyah, moh-lyah!

MORE...

What is the time?
Колко е часът?
Kol-koh eh chah-suht?

The time is:
Часът е:
Chah-suht eh:

half past two
два и половина
dvah ih poh-loh-vih-nah

quarter to three
три без петнадесет
trih bez pet-nah-deh-set

ten to eight
осем без десет
oh-sem bez deh-set

five past three
три и пет
trih ih pet

44

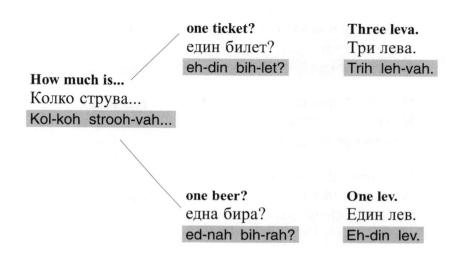

one ticket?
един билет?
eh-din bih-let?

Three leva.
Три лева.
Trih leh-vah.

How much is...
Колко струва...
Kol-koh strooh-vah...

one beer?
една бира?
ed-nah bih-rah?

One lev.
Един лев.
Eh-din lev.

AND MORE...

How old are you?
На **колко** години си/сте?
Nah-kol-koh goh-dih-nih sih/steh?

I am 25.
На двадесет и пет съм.
Nah dvah-deh-set ih pet suhm.

I am 50 years old.
Аз съм на петдесет години.
Az suhm nah pet-deh-set goh-dih-nih.

38
На тридесет и осем.
Nah trih-deh-set ih oh-sem.

How many houses do you have?
Колко къщи имате?
Kol-koh kuhsh-tih ih-mah-teh?

Two houses.
Две къщи.
Dveh kuhsh-tih.

How much money do you have?
Колко пари имаш?
Kol-koh pah-rih ih-mash?

Not much.
Не много.
Neh mnoh-goh.

How much do you love me?
Колко ме обичаш?
Kol-koh meh oh-bih-chash?

A lot!
Много!
Mnoh-goh!

READ ME!

The time

Forming the time in Bulgarian is very similar to English.

Forming the round hours:
Put the appropriate number in front of the word " часа", meaning hour:

Един часа - One O'clock

Четири часа - Four O'clock

Minutes past the hour:

From Bulgarian these literally translate:

(Hour) AND (the minutes)

(Три) и (десет) - three and ten = ten past three

Half past the hour:

In Bulgarian you say (Hour) AND (half):
Десет **и** половина - Ten and a half = half past ten

Minutes to the hour:

In Bulgarian, the minutes to the hour are taken away from the hour. It literally translates:

(hour) without/minus (the minutes)

Девет **без** петнадесет- Nine **without** fifteen =quarter to nine

Осем **без** двадесет и три - Eight **without** twenty three = twenty three minutes to eight

Listening exercises. (CD only)

LESSON 6

In the restaurant

Dialogue 1

Good evening! Can we have a table for two, please?
Добър вечер! Може ли маса за двама, моля!
Doh-buhr veh-cher! Moh-jeh lih mah-sah zah dvah-mah, moh-lyah!

There you are!
Заповядайте!
Zah-poh-vyah-dayh-teh!

Can we have the menu?
Може ли менюто?
Moh-jeh lih meh-niuh-toh?

Certainly!
Разбира се!
Raz-bih-rah seh!

Two cold beers, please.
Две студени бири, ако обичате!
Dveh stooh-deh-nih bih-rih, ah-koh oh-bih-chah-teh!

No problems.
Няма проблеми!
Nyah-mah prob-leh-mih!

There you go. Cheers!
Заповядайте! Наздраве!
Zah-poh-vyah-dayh-teh! Nah-zdrah-veh!

Thank you! Cheers!
Благодаря! Наздраве!
Blah-goh-dah-ryah! Nah-zdrah-veh!

Dialogue 2

Excuse me, can I have the bill!
Извинете, може ли сметката!
Iz-vih-neh-teh, moh-jeh lih smet-kah-tah!

Yes, just a moment! 15 leva, please!
Да, един момент! 15/петнадесет/ лева, моля!
Dah, eh-din moh-ment! Pet-nah-deh-set leh-vah, moh-lyah!

Do you accept credit cards?
Приемате ли кредитни карти?
Prih-eh-mah-teh lih kreh-dit-nih kar-tih?

No, I am sorry!
Не, съжалявам!
Neh, suh-jah-lyah-vam!

Here you go! Keep the change!
Заповядайте! Задръжте рестото!
Zah-poh-vyah-dayh-teh! Zah-druhj-teh res-toh-toh!

Thank you! Did you like the meal?
Благодаря! Хареса ли Ви яденето?
Blah-goh-dah-ryah! Hah-reh-sah lih Vih yah-deh-neh-toh?

Yes, it was wonderful!
Да, беше чудесно!
Dah, beh-sheh chooh-des-noh!

Where is the toilet, please?
Къде е толетната, моля?
Kuh-deh eh toh-ah-let-nah-tah, moh-lyah?

The second door to the right!
Втората врата вдясно!
Vtoh-rah-tah vrah-tah vdyas-noh!

Thank you! Have a nice evening! See you!
Благодаря! Приятна вечер! Довиждане!
Blah-goh-dah-ryah! Prih-yat-nah veh-cher! Doh-vij-dah-neh!

MORE...

Breakfast:
Закуска:
Zah-koohs-kah

coffee, banitsa
кафе, баница
kah-feh, bah-nih-tsah

Lunch:
Обяд:
Oh-byad

soup, tarator
супа, таратор
sooh-pah, tah-rah-tor

Supper/Dinner:
Вечеря:
Veh-cheh-ryah

mixed grill
мешана скара
meh-shah-nah skah-rah

I am a vegetarian.
Аз съм   вегетарианец
Az suhm veh-geh-tah-rih-
ah-nets.

I don't smoke.
Аз не пуша.
Az neh pooh-shah.

Non-smoking!
Тук не се пуши!
Tuk neh seh pooh-shih!

51

магданоз

Домат

Шопска салата

чушка

краставица

сирене

лук

Мешана скара

кебапче

кюфте

шишче

пържола

Гроздова ракия

пържени картофи

голяма гроздова

AND MORE...

Do you have...
Имате ли...
Imah-teh lih...

shopska salad?
шопска салата?
shop-skah sah-lah-tah?

chips?
пържени картофи?
puhr-jeh-nih kar-toh-fih?

beef steak?
телешка пържола?
teh-lesh-kah puhr-joh-lah?

cabbage salad?
салата от зеле?
sah-lah-tah ot zeh-leh?

fish?
риба?
rih-bah?

sandwiches?
сандвичи?
sand-vih-chih?

Can I have...
Може ли...
Moh-jeh lih...

the menu,
менюто,
meh-niuh-toh,

the salt,
солта,
sol-tah,

a glass of water,
чаша вода,
chah-shah voh-dah,

please!
моля!
moh-lyah!

Would you give me...
Дайте ми...
Daih-teh mih...

more bread,
още хляб,
osh-teh Hlyab,

one more beer
още една бира,
osh-teh ed-nah
bih-rah,

the bill,
сметката,
smet-kah-tah,

I want...
Искам...
Is-kam...

to order a taxi.
да поръчам такси.
dah poh-ruh-cham tak-sih.

to eat!
да ям!
dah yam!

54

READ ME!

"Заповядайте!"

The word **"Заповядай/-те"** is used in the following ways:

Заповядай/-те - as in: please; help yourself; in offering something and an invitation:

> Заповядай/-те, вземете си от тортата!
> Please help yourself to some cake!
>
> Заповядай/-те на гости! - Please come to visit!
>
> Заповядай/-те, влезте! - Please come in!

Заповядай/-те - as in: "there you go" and "here you are", when giving something to someone, often prompts the reply "Благодаря" - Thank you!

> A: Заповядай/-те рестото!
> There you go, here is your change
>
> B: Благодаря. - Thank you.

The very polite way of offering and inviting in Bulgarian is: **Моля заповядай/-те!**

Negative forms

In Bulgarian, you form negative sentences in the following ways:

With the negative particle "не" - used in front of the verb in the sentence, it turns it into a negative one:

> Аз пуша.- Аз **не** пуша. - I smoke. I don't smoke.

> Ние сме нови приятели - Ние **не** сме нови приятели

> We are new friends. - We are not new friends.

With "Няма", the negative form of the word "Има"

In sentences, where the word "**Има**" - ("there is" or "have") is present or implied, we form the negative sentence by swapping it with the word "**Няма**".

> Аз **имам** много пари - Аз **нямам** много пари.
> I have got lots of money. - I haven't got lots of money.

> **Има** проблеми - **Няма** проблеми.
> There are problems. - There are no problems.

Listening exercises. (CD only)

LESSON 7

In the bank

Dialogue 1

Good afternoon!
Добър ден!
Doh-buhr den!

Good afternoon! I want to open a bank account!
Добър ден! Искам да си отворя банкова сметка!
Doh-buhr den! Is-kam da sih ot-voh-ryah ban-koh-vah smet-kah!

Just a moment! Fill this in, please!
Един момент! Попълнете това, моля!
Eh-din moh-ment! Poh-puhl-neh-teh toh-vah, moh-lyah!

Like this?
Така ли?
Tah-kah lih?

Yes, that's right! What amount will you be depositing?
Да, точно така! Каква сума ще внесете?
Dah, toch-noh tah-kah! Kak-vah sooh-mah shteh vneh-seh-teh?

Two hundred pounds.
Двеста паунда.
Dves-tah pah-oohn-dah.

Dialogue 2

Excuse me, I want to exchange a hundred pounds?
Извинете, искам да обменя сто паунда!
Iz-vih-neh-teh, is-kam dah ob-meh-nyah stoh pah-oohn-dah!

No problems. The rate today is two leva and seventy stotinki /2.70/
Няма проблеми! Курсът днес е два лева и
седемдесет стотинки /2.70/
Nyah-mah prob-leh-mih! Koohr-sut dnes eh dvah leh-vah ih seh-dem-deh-set stoh-tin-kih.

OK. There you go!
Добре. Заповядайте!
Dob-reh. Zah-poh-vyah-dayh-teh!

There is your money for you. Have a nice day!
Ето Ви парите! Приятен ден!
Etoh vih pah-rih-teh! Prih-yah-ten den!

Thank you, you too.
Благодаря! И на вас!
Blah-goh-dah-ryah! Ih nah vas!

MORE...

I want water!
Искам вода!
Is-kam voh-dah!

Can I have a glass of water?
Може ли една чаша вода?
Moh-jeh lih ed-nah chah-shah voh-dah?

I want to smoke!
Искам да пуша!
Is-kam dah pooh-shah!

Can I smoke?
Може ли да пуша?
Moh-jeh lih dah pooh-shah?

I want to kiss you.!
Искам да те целуна!
Is-kam dah teh tseh-looh-nah!

Can I kiss you?
Може ли да те целуна?
Moh-jeh lih dah teh tseh-looh-nah?

I want to exchange some money!
Искам да обменя пари!
Is-kam dah ob-meh-nyah pah-rih!

Can I ask you to...?
Мога ли да Ви помоля...?
Moh-gah lih dah vih poh-moh-lyah?

Would you like anything else?
Желаете ли още нещо?
Jeh-lah-eh-teh lih osh-teh nesh-toh?

I want another/one more/ beer!
Искам още една бира!
Is-kam osh-teh ed-nah bih-rah!

AND MORE...

...numbers...

100 - сто /stoh/

101 - сто и едно /stoh ih ed-noh/

102 - сто и две /stoh ih dveh/

120 - сто и двадесет /stoh ih dvah-deh-set/

130 - сто и тридесет /stoh ih trih-deh-set/

200 - двеста /dveh-stah/

210 - двеста и десет /dveh-stah ih deh-set/

300 - триста /trih-stah/

350 - триста и петдесет /trih-stah ih pet-deh-set/

400 - четиристотин /cheh-tih-rih-stoh-tin/

500 - петстотин /pet-stoh-tin/

1000 - хиляда /Hih-lyah-dah/

1001 - хилядя и едно /Hih-lyah-dah ih ed-noh/

1020 - хиляда и двадесет /Hih-lyah-dah ih dvah-deh-set/

1200 - хиляда и двеста /Hih-lyah-dah ih dveh-stah/

4000 - четири хиляди /cheh-tih-rih Hih-lyah-dih/

10 000 - десет хиляди /deh-set Hih-lyah-dih/

20 000 - двадесет хиляди /dvah-deh-set Hih-lyah-dih/

150 000 - сто и петдесет хиляди /stoh ih pet-deh-set Hih-lyah-dih/

READ ME!

Forming numbers:

Round numbers 100- 1000

Round numbers 200 & 300 are formed as in English:

(small number) + the word "**ста**", derived from "**сто**"- 100.

200 - две-**ста**

300 - три-**ста**

The next round numbers are formed in the following manner:
(Small number)+ the word "**стотин**"- derived from "**сто**"- 100

400 -четири-**стотин**

700 - седем-**стотин**

Interim numbers are formed like in English:

306 - триста-**и**-шест

605 - шестотин-**и**-пет

The greater interim numbers come unchanged, after the big round hundred number:

564 - петстотин- шестдесет-**и**-четири.

987 - деветстотин-осемдесет-**и** седем

Round numbers - 1000 - 1,000,000

Formed like in English:

(small) +("**хиляди**") - pl. for "**хиляда**" 1000

3000 - три- **хиляди**

64000 - шестдесет и четири хиляди

Interim numbers 1000 - 1,000,000

These are formed just like in English.

Listening exercises. (CD only)

LESSON 8

At the estate agent

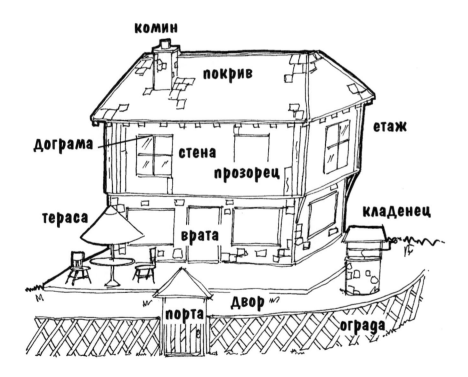

Dialogue 1

Hello! Good morning. I am looking for Krasi.
Ало! Добро утро. Търся Краси.
Aloh! Dob-roh ooht-roh! Tuhr-syah Krah-sih.

I am Krasi. Who is calling?
Аз съм Краси. Кой се обажда?
Az suhm Krah-sih. Koyh seh oh-baj-dah?

My name is Jane Smith and I am from England.
Аз се казвам Джейн Смит и съм от Англия!
Az seh kaz-vam Jane Smith ih suhm ot An-glih-yah!

Hi! How can I help you?
Здравейте! Как мога да Ви помогна?
Zdrah-veyh-teh! Kak moh-gah dah vih poh-mog-nah?

What properties do you have on offer?
Какви имоти имате?
Kak-vih ih-moh-tih ih-mah-teh?

We have all sorts of properties: houses, apartments...
Имаме различни имоти: къщи, апартаменти...
Ih-mah-meh raz-lich-nih ih-moh-tih: kuhsh-tih,
ah-par-tah-men-tih...

Where are they situated?
Къде се намират?
Kuh-deh seh nah-mih-rat?

We have some near the sea, as well as in land.
Имаме на морето и в страната.
Imah-meh nah moh-reh-toh ih v strah-nah-tah.

What are they like?
Какви са?
Kak-vih sah?

There are big and small ones, new and old ones.
Има големи и малки, нови и стари.
Imah goh-leh-mih ih mal-kih, noh-vih ih stah-rih.

Do you sell land?
Продавате ли земя?
Proh-dah-vah-teh lih zeh-myah?

Yes, we have plots too.
Да, имаме и парцели.
Dah, ih-mah-meh ih par-tseh-lih.

Thank you! Speak to you later!
Благодаря! Дочуване!
Blah-goh-dah-ryah! Doh-chuh-vah-neh!

Dialogue 2

The Viewing

This is the house. It was built 50 years ago.
Това е къщатата. Строена е преди 50 години.
Toh-vah eh kuhsh-tah-tah. Stroh-eh-nah eh preh-dih
pet-deh-set goh-dih-nih.

It's nice. How many rooms does it have?
Хубава е. Колко стаи има?
Hooh-bah-vah eh. Kol-koh stah-ih ih-mah?

There are four rooms: living room, kitchen, two bedrooms and a corridor.

Има четири стаи: хол, кухня, две спални
и коридор.

Imah cheh-tih-rih stah-ih: hohl, kooh-nyah, dveh spal-nih
ih koh-rih-dohr.

The toilet is outside, but it is possible to build one inside.

Тоалетната е от вън, но може да се направи
вътре.

Toh-ah-let-nah-tah eh ot vuhn , noh moh-jeh dah seh
nap-rah-vih vuht-reh!

Is it solid?

Стабилна ли е?

Stah-bil-nah lih eh?

**Yes, the walls are solid, the roof is strong,
the floor is concrete.**

Да, стените са солидни, покривът е здрав,
подът е циментов.

Dah, steh-nih-teh sah soh-lid-nih, pok-rih-vuht eh zdrav,
poh-duht eh tsih-men-tov.

How big is the yard?

Колко голям е дворът?

Kol-koh goh-lyam eh dvoh-ruht?

The yard is two acres, there is a vineyard of 200 sqm.

Дворът е два декара, има лозе 200 - двеста
квадратни метра.

Dvoh-ruht eh dvah deh-kah-rah, ih-mah loh-zeh
dves-tah kvad-rat-nih met-rah.

I like it, but it needs refurbishing.
Харесва ми, но има нужда от ремонт.
Hah-res-vah mih, noh ih-mah noohj-dah ot reh-mont.

No problems. We have builders.
Няма проблеми. Ние имаме строители.
Nyah-mah prob-leh-mih. Nieh imah-meh stroh-ih-teh-lih!

Is it going to be expensive?
Скъпо ли ще е?
Skuh-poh lih shteh eh?

Should be all right!
Ще се разберем!
Shteh seh raz-beh-rem!

This sounds good!
Това звучи добре!
Toh-vah zvooh-chih dob-reh!

MORE...

The house
Къщата
Kuhsh-tah-tah

The roof
Покривът
Pok-rih-vuht

The floor
Подът
Poh-duht

is in need of refurbishment.
има нужда от ремонт.
ih-mah noohj-dah ot reh-mont.

I'm looking for...
Търся...
Tuhr-syah...

a house	**near**	**the sea.**
къща	близо до морето.	
kuh-shtah	blih-zoh doh moh-reh-toh.	

a villa	**in**	**the mountains.**
вила	в	планината.
vih-lah	v	plah-nih-nah-tah.

a plot	**for**	**building.**
парцел	за	строеж.
par-tsel	zah	stroh-ej.

an apartment	**in**	**a resort.**
апартамент	в	курорт.
ah-par-tah-ment	v	kooh-rohrt.

Needed are:
Трябват:
Tryab-vat:

identification documents,
лични документи,
lich-nih doh-kooh-men-tih,

preliminary contract,
предварителен договор,
pred-vah-rih-teh-len doh-goh-vor,

10 percent deposit,
10/десет/ процента депозит,
deh-set proh-tsen-tah deh-poh-zit,

Needed are:
Трябват:
Tryab-vat:

> **own firm,**
> собствена фирма,
> sob-stveh-nah fir-mah,
>
> **valid title deeds,**
> валиден нотариален акт,
> vah-lih-den noh-tah-rih-ah-len akt,
>
> **independent solicitor,**
> независим адвокат,
> neh-zah-vih-sim ad-voh-kat,
>
> **certified power of attorney letter.**
> заверено пълномощно.
> zah-veh-reh-noh puhl-noh-mosht-noh.

AND MORE...

The apartment is expensive.
Апартаментът е скъп.
Ah-par-tah-men-tuht eh skuhp.

> **The plot is cheap.**
> Парцелът е евтин.
> Par-tseh-luht eh ev-tin.

The yard is big.
Дворът е голям.
Dvoh-ruht eh goh-lyam.

The house is on two floors.
Къщата е на два етажа.
Kuhsh-tah-tah eh nah dvah eh-tah-jah.

There is no bathroom.
Няма баня.
Nyah-mah bah-nyah.

There is a vineyard.
Има лозе.
Ih-mah loh-zeh.

The floor is wooden.
Подът е дървен.
Poh-duht eh duhr-ven.

There is an asphalt road.
Има асфалтов път.
Ih-mah as-fal-tov puht.

What percentage commission do you take?
Какъв процент комисионна вземате?
Kah-kav proh-tsent koh-mih-sih-on-nah vzeh-mah-teh?

How much will it cost for you to fix my roof?
Колко ще струва да ми поправите покрива?
Kol-koh shteh strooh-vah dah mih pop-rah-vih-teh pok-rih-vah?

READ ME!

Forming questions:

In Bulgarian language questions are usually formed in the following ways:

1. With a question word

Кой? -	Who?	Кога? -	When?
Как? -	How?	Къде? -	Where?
Какво? -	What?	Защо? -	Why?

These are usually in the beginning of the sentence and are used similarly as in the English language.

Or

2. Using the particle" ли" - which is the question word applied, to make a question sentence. In this way, we form questions, which can be answered with a "Yes" or a "No". The particle "ли" goes immediately after the word or words, which the question is about:

Болен съм. - I am ill.

> Болен **ли** си? Are you ill?

Добре сте. -You are well.

> Добре **ли** сте? - Are you well?

Ти си Българин - You are Bulgarian.

> Българин **ли** си? - Are you Bulgarian?

Listening exercises. (CD only)

74

LESSON 9

In the village

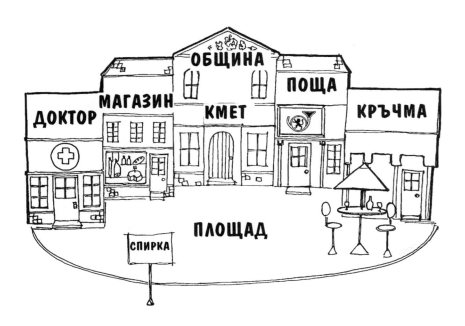

Dialogue 1

Good morning. Excuse me, where is the Parish office?
Добро утро! Извинете, къде е общината?
Dob-roh ooht-roh! Iz-vih-neh-teh, kuh-deh eh
ob-shtih-nah-tah?

In the square.
На площада.
Nah plosh-tah-dah.

Who is the mayor?
Кой е кметът?
Koyh eh kmeh-tuht?

Dimitar Ivanov. (His name)
Димитър Иванов.
Dih-mih-tuhr Ih-vah-nov.

When is he at work?
Кога е на работа?
Koh-gah eh nah rah-boh-tah?

On Monday, Wednesday and Thursday.
В понеделник, сряда и четвъртък.
V poh-neh-del-nik, sryah-dah ih chet-vuhr-tuhk.

Thank you!
Благодаря!
Blah-goh-dah-rya!

Is there a doctor in the village?
Има ли доктор в селото?
Ih-mah lih dok-tor v seh-loh-toh?

Yes, Dr. Petrov comes every Tuesday and Friday.
Да, Доктор Петров идва всеки вторник и петък.
Dah, Dok-tor Pet-rov id-vah vseh-kih vtor-nik ih peh-tuhk.

Dialogue 2

Neighbours

Hi, Ivan.
Здравей, Иване!
Zdrah-veyh, Ih-vah-neh!

Hi, Jane! Welcome back!
When did you arrive from England?
Здрасти, Джейн! Добре дошли!
Кога пристигнахте от Англия?
Zdras-tih, Jane! Dob-reh doh-shlih!
Koh-gah pris-tihg-nah-teh ot An-glih-yah?

Late last night. How are you, lot?
Късно снощи. Вие как сте?
Kuhs-noh snoh-shtih. Vih-eh kak steh?

We are fine. Working in the garden.
Добре сме. Работим в градината.
Dob-reh smeh. Rah-boh-tim v grah-dih-nah-tah.

Come to visit us tonight.
Заповядайте на гости довечера.
Zah-poh-vyah-dayh-teh nah gos-tih doh-veh-cheh-rah.

There are presents for you!
Има подаръци за вас!
Imah poh-dah-ruh-tsih zah vas!

Thank you! What should we bring?
Благодаря! Ние какво да донесем?
Blah-goh-dah-ryah! Nih-eh kak-voh dah doh-neh-sem?

Bring some of your rakia. It is very nice.
Донесете от вашата ракия.Тя е много хубава!
Doh-neh-seh-teh ot vah-shah-tah rah-kih-yah.
Tyah eh mnoh-goh Hooh-bah-vah!

MORE...

Monday	Понеделник / poh-neh-del-nik /
Tuesday	Вторник / vtor-nik /
Wednesday	Сряда / sryah-dah /
Thursday	Четвъртък / chet-vuhr-tuhk /
Friday	Петък / peh-tuhk /
Saturday	Събота / suh-boh-tah /
Sunday	Неделя / neh-deh-lyah /

Where can I pay...
Къде мога да платя...
Kuh-deh moh-gah dah plah-tyah...

the electricity?
електричеството /тока/?
eh-lek-trih-ches-tvoh-toh /toh-kah/?

In the Council.
В общината.
V ob-shtih-nah-tah.

my tax?
таксата си?
tak-sah-tah sih?

In the post office.
В пощата.
V poh-shtah-tah.

Where can I pay the water bill?
Къде мога да платя сметката за водата?
Kuh-deh moh-gah dah plah-tyah smet-kah-tah
zah voh-dah-tah?

> **In the Council.**
> В съвета.
> V suh-veh-tah.

AND MORE...

How much for...
Колко ще струва...
Kol-koh shteh strooh-vah...

you to look after my house?
да се грижите за моята къща?
dah seh grih-jih-teh zah moh-yah-tah kuhsh-tah?

you to look after my garden?
да се грижиш за градината ми?
dah seh grih-jish zah grah-dih-nah-tah mih?

you to look after my keys?
да се грижиш за ключовете ми?
dah seh grih-jish zah kliuh-choh-veh-teh mih?

you to pay my bills?
да ми плащаш сметките?
dah mih plash-tash smet-kih-teh?

Could I ask...
Може ли...
Moh-jeh lih ...

READ ME!

Definite article

Unlike in English, the definite article in Bulgarian is not a separate word, but it appears as an ending to the noun. When in a sentence, there is an adjective describing the noun- the adjective carries the article.

The definite article is different in the three genders. Generally, they are formed like this:

When the noun is a subject in a sentence:

1) For masculine noun - add - **ът/-ят**

Агентът взе документите. - **The** agent took the documents.
Лекарят е много добър. - **The** Doctor is very good.

Otherwise:

For masculine nouns - add **-а / -я**
адвокат- адвоката, / майстор- майстора / лекар- лекаря

2) For feminine nouns- add **-та**
къща- къщата / вода- водата

3) For neuter nouns- add - **то**
дете- детето, / море- морето

Listening exercises. (CD only)

LESSON 10

The weather

Hello, Maria! Where are you calling from?
Ало, Мария! От къде се обаждаш?
Ah-loh! Mah-rih-yah! Ot kuh-deh seh oh-baj-dash?

From Varna. Do you hear me?
От Варна.Чуваш ли ме?
Ot Var-nah! Chooh-vash lih meh?

Yes, I hear you. How is the weather?
Да, чувам те. Как е времето?
Dah, chooh-vam teh. Kak eh vreh-meh-toh?

It's very warm today. Yesterday was cold.
Много е топло днес. Вчера беше студено.
Mnoh-goh eh top-loh dnes.Vcheh-rah beh-sheh stuh-deh-noh.

Tomorrow will be cloudy. And over by you?
Утре ще бъде облачно. А при теб?
Ooht-reh shteh buh-deh ob-lach-noh. Ah prih teb?

Today it's raining. Tomorrow will be windy.
Днес вали дъжд. Утре ще духа вятър.
Dnes vah-lih duhjd. Ooht-reh shteh duh-hah vyah-tuhr.

Yesterday was sunny.
Вчера беше слънчево.
Vcheh-rah beh-sheh sluhn-cheh-voh.

You know England!
Нали знаеш-Англия!
Nah-lih znah-esh- An-gih-yah!

What are you saying- it's snowing?
Какво казваш- вали сняг?
Kak-voh kaz-vash - vah-lih snyag?

No, it's raining! The weather is bad this month!
Не, вали дъжд! Времето е лошо този месец!
Neh, vah-lih duhjd! Vreh-meh- toh eh loh-shoh toh-zih
meh-sets!

It's hot here this week!
Тук е горещо тази седмица!
Toohk eh goh-reh-shtoh tah-zih sed-mih-tsah!

OK, Maria, speak to you later!
Добре Мария, дочуване!
Dob-reh Mah-rih-yah, doh-chooh-vah-neh!

No, I can't hear...!
Не, не чувам...!
Neh, neh chooh-vam...!

Dialogue 2

Hi, is this the new car?
Здравей, това ли е новата кола?
Zdrah-veyh, toh-vah lih eh noh-vah-tah koh-lah?

Yes!
Да!
Dah!

When did you buy it?
Кога я купи?
Koh-gah yah kooh-pih?

I saw it the day before yesterday, paid for it yesterday, took it today and I will drive it tomorrow.
Онзи ден я видях, вчера я платих, днес я взех, утре ще я карам!
On-zih den yah vih-dyah, vcheh-rah yah plah-tih, dnes yah vzeh, ooh-treh shteh yah kah-ram!

The day after I will sell it!
Други ден ще я продам.
Druh-gih den shteh yah proh-dam.

I have a new house!
Аз имам нова къща!
Az ih-mam noh-vah kuhsh-tah!

Really?
Така ли?
Tah-kah lih?

Yes, I chose it in March, bought it in May, now in June I am renovating it and in August I will sell it!
Да, през март я избрах, през май я купих, сега през юни я ремонтирам и през август ще я продам!
Dah, prez mart yah iz-brah, prez mayh yah kooh-pih, seh-gah prez iu-nih yah reh-mon-tih-ram ih prez av-gust shteh yah proh-dam.

Yesterday rained.
Вчера валя дъжд.
Vcheh-rah vah-lyah duhjd.

Today it's snowing.
Днес вали сняг.
Dnes vah-lih snyag.

Tomorrow will be sunny.
Утре ще грее слънце.
Ooht-reh shteh greh-eh sluhn-tseh.

The day after tomorrow will be cloudy.
В други ден ще бъде облачно.
V drooh-gih den shteh buh-deh ob-lach-noh.

This year is rainy.
Тази година е дъждовна
Tah-zih goh-dih nah eh duhj-dov-nah!

The weather is cold. It's cold.
Времето е студено. Студено е.
Vreh-meh-toh eh stuh-deh-noh. Stuh-deh-noh eh!

Wind is blowing. It's windy.
Духа вятър. Ветровито е!
Dooh-hah vyah-tuhr. Vet-roh-vih-toh eh!

The weather is hot. I am hot.
Времето е горещо! Горещо ми е!
Vreh-meh-toh eh goh-reh-shtoh! Goh-reh-shtoh mih eh!

AND MORE...

January	Януари /Yah-nooh-ah-rih/
February	Февруари /Fev-ruh-ah-rih/
March	Март /Mart/
April	Април /Ahp-ril/
May	Май /Mayh/
June	Юни /Iuh-nih/
July	Юли /Iuh-lih/
August	Август /Av-goohst/
September	Септември /Sep-tem-vrih/
October	Октомври /Ok-tom-vrih/
November	Ноември /Noh-em-vrih/
December	Декември /Deh-kem-vrih/

READ ME!

"Ще" - Forming future tense

To turn a sentence into future tense, simply put the word "**ще**" in front of the verb.

Лятото **е** горещо. - Лятото **ще е** горещо.
The summer is hot. - The summer will be hot.

Джон **учи** български - Джон **ще учи** български.
John studies Bulgarian - John will study Bulgarian.

Listening exercises. (CD only)

Dictionary

In this dictionary, you will find all Bulgarian words from the lessons in this book. They appear in the form in which you meet them in the text. This is followed by their form, in which you can find them in any dictionary: the verbs - in first person, singular; present, the adjectives - in masculine singular, although on occasions the three gender's endings are shown.

The English translation shows the meaning of the basic form.

A fully comprehensive interactive dictionary is provided in the second CD for your reference.

Abbreviations:

fm-from
f- feminine
m- masculine
n- neuter

pl- plural
s- singular
adj- adjective

The Bulgarian Alphabet

ало - hello (used in telephone conversations only)
апетит - appetite
Балкан - Balkan (the name for Stara Planina mountain)
бар - bar
вана - bath
вода - water
говоря - to talk
голям - big
да - yes, to (do something)
добре - well, good (adj)
ела / fm **идвам** / - to come
елен - reindeer

жена - woman
живот - life
земя - earth, land
зима - winter
има - there is/are
име - name
йод - iodine
Йордания - Jordan
какво - what
кога - when
леко - light (as in weight)
лято - summer
магазин - shop
мама - mum
не - no, (particle used to form negative sentences)
няма - there isn't (any)/ none

обичам - to love; to like
осем - eight
пари - money
пия - to drink
работа - work
радост - joy
слънце - sun
стая - room
това - this
толкова - so much; this much
урок - lesson
уча - to learn
фар - light house
финал - finale
хляб - bread
хубав/-а/-о - nice, pretty, good looking
цвете - flower
целувам - to kiss
червено - red
червило - lipstick
шофьор - driver
шунка - ham
щастие - happiness
ще - will (future tense particle)
ъгъл - corner, angle
юрист - lawyer, a law graduate
ябълка - apple
ям - to eat

Lesson 1

аз - I
ако обичате/fm обичам/ - if you would
англичанин(m) - an Englishman
англичанка(f) - an English woman
Англия - England
бавно - slow
благодаря - Thank you
българка - Bulgarian woman (f)
български/-а/-о - Bulgarian (adj)
България - Bulgaria
вечер - evening
вие (pl) - you
всичко - everything
всичко хубаво - all the best
герой - hero
ден - day
добре дошли! - welcome (here)
добро утро - good morning
добър/-а/-о - good, nice (adj)
добър вечер - good evening
добър ден - good afternoon
довиждане - good bye
дошли /fm идвам/- to come
здравей - hello
и - and
извинете - to excuse
казвам - to tell
казваш се/ fm казвам се/ - your /mine name is(I am called)
как - how
как си? -how are you?
къде - where
лека нощ- good night
майка - mother
маса - table
мен - me (dative)
много - very, many, much, a lot
моля - please

море - sea
мъж - a man
на - on, at, of, to, for / depends on the context/
не/разбирам - I don't understand(fm-разбирам)
но - but
нощ - night
от - from, (made) of, since
писмо - letter
приятна работа - have a good day at work
приятно/-а/ приятен/ - pleasant
приятно ми е - my pleasure
приятно прекарване - have a nice time
съм - am
такси - taxi
ти - you
утро - morning, dawn
чувствам - to feel

Lesson 2

дете - child
доктор - doctor
един - one
имам - to have
колега - colleague
коридор - corridor
къща - a house
легло - bed
ли - a question particle, used to form question sentences
ние - us
приятел/-и - friend/-s

семейство /-а - family/-s
спалня - double bed, bedroom
съсед/-и - neighbour /-s
също - as well, too, same as
така - like this
те -they
ти - you
той - he
то - it
турист - tourist
тя - she
уморен -/a/-о- tired
часа - /fm час/- hour; O' clock
чужденец - foreigner (m)
чужденка - foreigner (f)

Lesson 3

бира - beer
вино - wine
да мина /fm минавам/ - to get past / through
да питам/fm питам/ - to ask
да пушите /fm пуша/ - to smoke
да видя / fm виждам/ - to see
да шофира/fm шофирам/ - to drive
заедно - together
закуска - breakfast
заповядайте - welcome, please (as in inviting)
кашкавал - cheese (yellow)
кисело мляко - yoghurt
кремвирши - frankfurters
кутия - a box
лев - lev- the Bulgarian currency

луканка - lukanka- typical Bulgarian dried meat delicacy
мляко - milk
може - can, is able to, is permitted to
питам - to ask
по-късно - later
олио - oil
оцет - vinegar
стотинки - stotinki - the Bulgarian currency's small change; penny, cent
струва - cost
суджук - sujuck- typical Bulgarian meat delicacy
тук - here
целуна /fm целувам/ - to kiss
цигара/-и - cigarette/s

Lesson 4

банка - bank
близо - near, close
боли (ме) - hurt (me), to hurt
в - in
вечеряме /fm вечерям/ - to have dinner/supper; to dine
внимание - attention
върнете се обратно - go back / on your self/
върнете /fm връщам/ - to return
гара - station
далече - far
до - to, next to, until
дясно - right (as in direction)
за - for

завийте /fm завивам/ - to turn
края /fm край/ - end (the)
ляво - left
моля - please
на гърба/ fm гръб/ - at the back, back
надясно - to the right
наляво - to the left
намира (се) - to find; it's situated
направо - straight ahead
небе - sky
него - him (acc.)
не знам - I don't know
обратно - back, backwards, inside out, upside down, opposite
отсреща - opposite (here)
паркинг - car park, parking space
плаж - beach
помощ - help
поща - post, post office
пресечете /fm пресичам/ - to cross (the street)
продължете /fm продължавам/ - to continue
ресторант - restaurant
светофар -a - traffic light - the
след - after
срещу - opposite (something) against
стигна /fm стигам/ - to reach, to last, enough
точно - exact, precise
у дома - at home
улица-та - street (the)
успех - success

хотел - hotel

Lesson 5

без - without
билет - ticket
връщане /fm връщам (се)/ - return (to return)
глава-та - head (the)
година/-и - year/-s
готово - ready
дайте ми (fm давам) - give me (to give)
дължа - to owe
задръжте (fm задържам) - to keep, to withhold, to retain
колко? - how much/ many?
колко е часът? - What is the time?
малко - little, a little, small, few
отиване (fm отивам) - to go
пари - money
повторете (fm повтарям) - to repeat
половин - half
рейс-ът - bus (the)
ресто-то - change (the) / as in the money difference due back/
само - only
свободен - free (not engaged), liberated
сега - now
спрете (fm спирам) - to stop
със & с - with (със- is used in front of words, starting with an "с" or a "з")

Lesson 6

баница -a typical Bulgarian pastry dish
беше /fm съм/ - (was)- to be
вегетарианец - a vegetarian
вечеря - supper
вземете си (fm взимам) - to take (take some!)
влезте (fm влизам) - то enter, to come in (come in!)
гроздов/-а/-о - made of grapes
двама (fm два) - two - for people
домат - tomato
зеле - cabbage
картоф/и- potato/es
кафе - coffee
кебапче - typcal Bulgarian mince meet finger
краставица - cucumber
кредитна/-и карта/-и (pl)/ - credit card/s
кюфте - typcal Bulgarian mince meet ball
лук - onion
магданоз - parsley
меню-то - menu (the)
мешана скара - mixed grill
момент - moment
наздраве - cheers (only used as salute when drinking alchoholic beverages)
нов/-и - new (pl)
обяд - lunch
поръчам (fm поръчвам) - то order

проблем/-и - problem/-s

примате (fm приемам) -то accept

пържени- fried

пържени картофи - chips

пържола - steak

разбира (се) (fm разбирам) - of course (to understand)

риба - fish

сандвич/-и - sandwich/es

сметка-та - bill (the), account (bank)

сол-та - salt (the)

студен/-и - cold (pl)

супа - soup

съжалявам - to be sorry, to regret

таратор - Bulgarian summer cold soup type dish

телешко - beef

телешка пържола - beef steak

тоалетна - toilet

торта-та - cake (the)

хареса / fm харесвам/ - to like, to fancy

чаша - cup, glass (as in container)

чушка -a pepper

шишче -Bulgarian meet skewers

шопска салата - a famous Bulgarian salad dish

Lesson 7

банков/-а/-о - bank's

внесете /fm внасям/ - to bring in, to deposite

желаете ли? /fm желая/ - would you like? (would like to), to want

курс-ът - exchange rate, course (the)

нали - untranslatable, used to invite agreement and confirmation, tag question word

обменя/fm обменям/ - to exchange(i.e. currency)

отворя/fm отварям/ - to open

още - more

паунд/-а - pound/-s

помоля /fm моля/ - to ask for, to begg

попълнете/fm попълвам/ - to fill out/in

нещо - something

сума - amount

това - this

Lesson 8

апартамент/-и - apartment/-s, flats

баня - bathroom

болен - ill, sick

врата - door

вън - out, outdoors

вътре - inside, indoors

големи (pl) - big

декар/-а - 1000 sqm

двор - yard, garden

дограма - joinery work

днес - today

дочуване /fm чувам/ - speak to you again; /to hear/

дървен/а/о - wooden

евтин/-а/-о - cheap
етаж - floor (as in 1st, 2nd)
звучи /fm звуча/ - to sound
здрав - not broken, in good condition, healthy
имот/и - property/ies
квадратни - square (pl) (adj)
кладенец - well (water)
комин - chimney
кухня - kitchen
лозе - vineyard
малки - small (pl)
направи /fm правя/ - to make, to do
нужда - need (noun)
нужда от ремонт - need of refurbishment
обажда /fm обаждам се/ - to call (on the telephone)
облачно - cloudy, overcast
ограда - fence
от вън - outside
парцел/-и - plot/-s
под-ът - floor (the)
помогна /fm помагам/ - to help
покрив - ът- roof (the)
порта - porch
прекрасно - marvelous
продавате /fm продавам/ - to sell
процент - percent
разберем /fm разбирам (се)/ - to reach an agreement; to understand
различни - different (pl)
ремонт - refurbishment

скъпо - expensive, treasured, dear
спалня/-и (pl) - bedroom/s, double bed/s
стабилна - solid, sturdy
стар/и - old
стена - wall
стени-те - walls (the) (pl)
страна-та - country (the), side
строена /fm строя/ - built /to build/
строител/-и - builder/-s
тераса - terrace, patio
търся - to look for
хол - living room
циментов - made of cement

Lesson 9

агент-ът - agent (the)
адвокат - solicitor, lawyer
ваша-та - yours (f)
взе /fm вземам/ - to take
всеки - every one, each one
гост/-и - guest/-s, visitor/-s
градина-та - garden (the)
грижите /fm грижа (се)/ - to take care of (pl)
да донесем /fm донасям/ - to bring
довечера - tonight, this evening
документи-те - documents (the)
електричество-то; ток-а - both words for electricity (the)
идва /fm идвам/ - to come
ключове-те - keys (the)

кмет-а - mayor (the)
кръчма - pub
късно - late
лекар - doctor
магазин - shop
майстор - handyman, tradesman
мога - can
община-та - council office (the)
плащаш /fm плащам/ - to pay
площад-а - town square (the)
пристигнахте / fm **пристигам/** - to arrive
работа - work
работим /fm работя/ - to work
ракия - rakiya- Bulgarian grape brandy
село-то - village (the)
снощи - last night
спирка - bus stop
съвет-а - parish council (the)
такса-та - tax (the)

Lesson 10

валя /fm вали/ - to rain or to snow. It needs another word to be either.
ветровито - windy
взех /fm вземам/ - to take
видях /fm виждам/ - to see
време - то- weather (the)
вчера - yesterday
вятър - wind
горещо - hot
грее - to shine, to release heat
други ден - the day after tomorrow

избрах /fm избирам/ - chose, to choose
карам - driving a vehicle; making someone to do something
кола - car
купи /fm купувам/ - to buy
лош/-а/-о - bad
месец - month
нали знаеш - as you know, you know
онзи - the other
онзи ден - the other day, the day before yesterday
през - through, during
при - by (someone or somewhere) at someone's end
ремонтирам - to refurbish
седмица - week
сняг - snow
студено - cold
теб /fm ти/ - you
този - this one
топло - warm
утре - tomorrow
чуваш /fm чувам/ - to hear
ще бъде - will be
я /fm тя/ - she

Lyrics: G. Konstantinov
Music: A. Miladinov
Vocals: Marinella Pashova
The sound track to the bellow lyrics can be found at the end of CD2. Enjoy!

Чувство

Сред жадните дюни цъфти
невиждана пясъчна лилия.
Отдавна я търсеше ти -
отново те питам - откри ли я?

Щом можеш и миг ти без мен -
не вярвам на други мигове,
щом можеш без мен и ден -
ще можеш без мен и винаги...

Спокойна си тръгвам сега
под крясък на гладни гларуси,
далече от мойта тъга,
далече от твойте радости.

Отивам си с тих послеслов -
дори и не правя усилие,
да търся във тебе любов
и в пясъка - пясъчна лилия.

Щом можеш и миг ти без мен -
не вярвам на други мигове
щом можеш без мен и ден -
ще можеш без мен и винаги...

Спокойна си тръгвам сега
под крясък на гладни гларуси,
далече от мойта тъга,
далече от твойте радости.

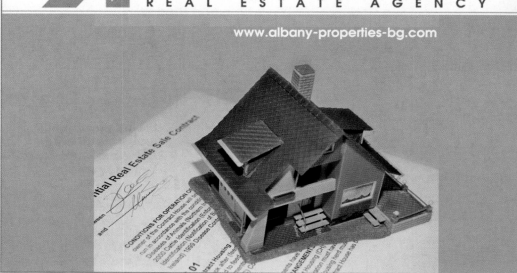